Contents

5   Baseball Strategies for the Workplace

11   Watch your assumptions: They might lead you down the wrong path

15   Shotgun or Rifle Approach? It all Depends upon your Perspective

18   Don't "Strike Out" in the Interview Process

24   3 Leadership traits to embrace when the time is right

27   You have to keep learning

32   Your most important network

36   From Telescopes to Microscopes, Great Leaders need it all

42   Your Web of Inclusion-Who is there?

46   Have you assumed the correct Leadership Position?

50   Gaining Wisdom from Others-The Art of Listening

57	Putting the Pieces into Place-The Challenge of Networking
62	Don't let a First Impression Sidetrack a Potential Connection
66	The Best Talent Development Opportunities may Surprise you
71	Are you a Chronos or Kairos Leader?

Foreword

I have had the dream of writing a book for years. I cannot tell you how many times I have gotten started, only to get distracted and then let the project drop.

The content of this book is the culmination of a number of writings I have had over the past 3 years while feeding my blog, The Search for Authentic Leadership. I find my writing to be somewhat therapeutic in nature and most of what I write about fits in to the areas of leadership, networking and relationships within the workplace and my family.

There are several people I need to thank for their support and inspiration. First, I have to thank my wife, Gena, and my sons, Daniel and Matthew, for their constant support, encouragement and feedback (mostly positive). I also must give credit to the pastors I have learned so much from, namely David Cassidy, Tony Giles and Scotty Smith. I also need to give credit to my in-laws, Sue and Lamon Lovett. I have been so blessed to have them as friends, relatives and wise counsel for over 34 years.

You will see a number of interests in my writing, especially my love for college baseball, specifically the Vanderbilt Commodores.

To all of these I dedicate this work.

Baseball Strategies for the Workplace

As a fan of college baseball and specifically the Vanderbilt Commodores I find it quite easy to use baseball as a metaphor for life. On this morning after the final game of the College World Series I feel compelled to write briefly about how the game of baseball mirrors working in teams in most of the organizations I have been a part of. While you may not see all of the parallels I see, I hope you find the comparisons to be of interest and value to you.

Baseball has a number of strategic plays that have strong resemblance to what goes on in the world of work. I'll describe 3 for you here and draw analogies about how they relate to work.

Sacrifice Bunt or Sacrifice Fly

The sacrifice is a play where the batter intentionally hits the ball in a manner to advance a runner who happens to be on base. This play, bunt or fly ball, is intended to advance the team and the batter has full recognition that he/she will not personally benefit, but that the team will benefit from his/her action.

Leaders in organizations often have opportunities to make strategic or tactical moves that will advance those who he/she leads or works with. It is rare to see a leader who is willing to do this on a regular basis unless the culture of the team recognizes and rewards this type of unselfish behavior. If an organization fully appreciates how one can advance another by putting them in a position to "score", then the entire organization can adopt a set of tactics that will advance the entire group while not focusing more on individual accomplishment. It is truly a mature and advanced organizational culture that embraces the sacrificial play.

Backing up the play

When a play is being made and one player throw the ball to another, one of the players closest to the play may back up the throw or may back up the player fielding the ball. The purposes of backing up a player is to prevent the ball from getting loose and allowing the opposing team to advance if the ball is not fielded cleanly or if the throw is errant.

Organizations and their players need back up in most everything that happens. When you back up your co-worker the intent should not be to find fault, but to help them be successful. By providing back up it helps the entire team and also allows those making the play to attempt to make the best play possible. Without trust that there is someone backing you up, the player making the play may not take the appropriate risk needed to either field the ball cleanly or to make a throw on a timely basis. Backing one another up in the workplace is fundamental tactic that can be the crucial difference between good cohesion and team success.

Going to the bullpen

In baseball there are times when the manager needs to bring in another pitcher to help keep the opposing team from scoring more runs. The relief pitcher may come in for just one batter or he/she may be in for the duration; it just depends upon the situation.

Organizations too should have a bullpen where they have players ready to step in when the situation dictates. One of the challenges that I have seen in organizations I have worked for as well as ones I have worked with is that they don't have sufficient depth in their bullpen or on their bench. When this happens there is no one to turn to when times get tough. In addition, younger or less experienced players either get no relevant experience or get "thrown into the fire" because they have to deal with issues they are not ready for. Either way is bad for the team.

Baseball is much like life. Both are full of strategies that lead to tactical decisions that either help or hinder the progress of the team and the organization as a whole. Understanding the concept of the sacrifice, backing up and the bullpen can mean the difference between success and failure. I would encourage you to see how you can incorporate each of these into your team and your organization. The difference will be measurable and long-lasting.

Watch your assumptions: They might lead you down the wrong path

Assumptions are a necessary evil. We all have them and our thoughts, words and actions are guided by them, sometimes too much. I suspect you can never totally tune them out, and you should never do so completely, but they can be the beginning of problems when not couched with other input and feedback. If assumptions are such a challenge, then there should be ways to deal with them. Let's talk about that.

Our language is full of assumptions and we sometimes don't even know we are making them in what we do and say. Let me share a few examples that I have experienced:

- May I speak with the man of the house? Not sure that is safe in today's world.
- Get the right man for the job-with women continuing to join and grow their

knowledge and expertise in the <u>workforce</u> this is a really challenging phrase that sometimes slips out in conversations I hear.
- Will your husband/wife be joining you? Again, the world we live in has more unmarried couples living together than those who are married, so the word spouse is becoming a safer term to use, even the term partner.

Many of us also have built-in assumptions based on geography. There are those who think all southerners are backward and barefoot, but I swear I wear shoes most every day, really. Others make assumptions that everyone in Canada goes around saying "Aye" in every sentence. Wrong! Further, not everyone in Texas drives a SUV (but many do) and they don't all own guns. As a Christian, I sometimes believe that other faiths are not as "correct" as mine, but I have to remember that a person's belief is their own personal property and God will make the choice regarding who believes, not me. All I can do is share what He has done for me.

How does one go about using their assumptions to the best end? Here are a few suggestions that I try to employ:

- Do your homework before you communicate or meet with someone you do not know. This can be extremely helpful in so many ways. Knowing where someone grew up, what they have done, almost anything will make a valid difference in how you approach and address them.
- Western (American) customs are not necessarily the best to use when you are working with someone from outside the USA. I know that I have sometimes used

that imperialistic mind-set that causes others to see us as "ugly Americans" and the best experiences I have had outside the country have helped curb my approach to others who don't have the same conditioning that I have had.
- We all see the world through the lens of our experience. Be sure to know the refractive and magnification of your lenses. Doing so will keep you from quickly jumping to conclusions that could lead to awkward or even embarrassing situations.

The world, even our country, is a big place.

Remember what happens when you assume. Use more than your own lenses to judge a situation or others who are involved. You'll be glad you took the time to look at something from other perspectives.

It's time to go and head to my square dancing lesson. Some people think all of us here in Tennessee only line dance or square dance.

Shotgun or Rifle Approach?
It all Depends upon your Perspective

In growing a small business, I learn something new every day. One of the toughest things I have had to learn over and over is that in order to grow the business I need to "get out of the kitchen" and let others bake the cakes. I learned this metaphor well when I read the book "The E-myth revisited" a few years ago. Most entrepreneurs do many things well and as a result then have a challenge in giving up control as their business grows. This continues to be a painful process for yours truly.

As an entrepreneur I started my business with somewhat of a "shotgun" approach, working in a wide variety of markets doing whatever it took to grow the business and keep food on the table. God has continued to bless us well and I tell people things are fine because I still have the <u>same wife</u>, the same home and most of the same friends after being on the entrepreneurial journey for almost 10 years now. For all of these things I am immensely grateful.

As I continue to grow the business, I see more and more to take more of a "rifle approach" and focus in on doing a few things well versus trying to do everything well. This applies to me as a leader as well as the focus of the business. We have several core markets we address and our span has grown a little since the time we first started 9 years ago. We have also abandoned some markets upon realizing that we didn't have the right expertise to be the best, or one of the best, in those markets. My good friend, Marc Fortune, always shares with me that there are "riches in niches" and I try to keep this in mind as we move ahead.

Rifles and shotguns are both weapons, but their intent is very different. A shotgun is great when you want to spray a number of projectiles over a wide area. A rifle is better when you want to address one singular target with minimal disruption to the surroundings. As I continue this journey along the entrepreneurial road, I hope to take more of the rifle approach and concentrate our efforts on a few key areas versus trying to spread our firm too thin.

As an entrepreneur, do you see the same issue in your business?

Don't "Strike Out" in the Interview Process

For those of you who know me well you understand well that one of my great interests is College. Since 2007 I have been a season ticket holder of the Reigning National Champion Vanderbilt Commodore baseball team. Knowing this, it should come as no shock that I use a baseball metaphor to discuss one of the key components of a job search process, the interview. I'll spend some time today discussing how not to "strike out", meaning how you can avoid from failing in the process. This doesn't mean that you will never make a mistake, but my intent is to keep you from knocking yourself out of the process.

Each batter gets three strikes and I'll arrange my post today in the form of three strikes to avoid in the interview process. If things go well there may be a fourth strike allowed (from a foul ball; we certainly would not want to change the rules of the greatest game going).

Strike 1-Being unprepared for the interview

The first strike is always lack of preparation. It is so simple now to gather information about firms that you will be interviewing with. Why not do so? It makes a great impression to be able to share with the interview team what you have learned about their firm. Who knows, you might even share something you have read they are totally unaware of. Being prepared with knowledge about the firm and even more, about those you are interviewing with, will make a good first impression.

Strike 2-Having a poor resume

If you avoid the first strike, this second strike will possibly trip you up. In most cases, if your resume was not good, you would not even get to the interview, but there are times when your resume is still not good enough. Here are a few key items to keep in mind when crafting your resume:

- Make it orderly and easy to follow
- Imagine your resume is like a newspaper; put the most important items on the top of the fold on the first page-if that area is not intriguing, they will not get any farther anyway
- List accomplishments in quantitative and qualitative fashion; numerical growth, % improvement or % cost reduction; what gets measured, matters

- Avoid the cutesy paper and graphics unless you are applying for a very creative type of role
- No typos-Grammatically correct!
- at least 11 point font-no unusual fonts

<u>Strike 3-Answer the questions completely, but don't over answer</u>

I have this conversation often with candidates we prepare for our clients. When a client asks a question, answer it completely. Support the answer, especially if it is a behavioral question. Over answering can also be a problem. Unless the question is multi-faceted or extremely deep, don't over answer the question. Keep to the facts and be succinct whenever possible.

Strike 4-Be sure to thank the interviewers properly

Even though a batter gets just three strikes in the game, I will give you a fourth strike today. The interview is important, but what happens after the interview is just as important. Be sure to ask the interview team what the process will be for moving ahead and thank them while in the room. In the same day, be sure to email every person you spoke with to personally thank them for meeting with you. Within 24-36 hours, send a personal, hand-written, thank you note to at least the key members of the interview team, if not every member. In this high-tech world of today, the high-touch candidate will be remembered.

In baseball, three strikes will send you back to the bench. Avoid the items listed above and you will possibly make it to the next base and who knows, you may score during the next play.

Also remember this, even if you do strike out, go back and review what happened so you can do better the next time. In baseball, the best players in the game only get on base 3 or 4 times out of ten. Failure is part of the game and how you adapt and improve from that failure will be the difference between sitting on the bench and ending up on ESPN.

You hold your fate in your own hands.

3 Leadership traits to embrace when the time is right

Leadership is a word that is thrown around loosely by many. Most of us intuitively know what leadership is, and we also know what things are like when leadership is absent from a situation. While listening to another wonderful message from my pastor, David Cassidy, yesterday I thought that these three terms he used in his sermon might be good cornerstones for a short post on traits that leaders need to embrace when the situation is right.

- **Commission**
- **Submission**
- **Omission**

Let me dive a little deeper into each of these and the context of when to utilize them.

Leaders need to utilize Commission when the time to act is right. I have seen many circumstances where leaders have been afraid or wary of taking action, and it has been my experience that taking action is usually superior to not doing anything when a situation needs to be addressed. One of the most common areas to practice commission is when an employee needs to be redirected or given feedback. So often I see leaders let the incorrect behavior fester and provide a negative environment for those affected by the misbehaving person. Leaders need to commit to take action when the timing is appropriate. Waiting can be devastating for all involved.

Submission is a word I don't often see used when leadership is addressed, but leaders need to learn when to submit in a variety of instances. One of the traits I see few leaders employ is to submit to others when the other party has the ability to move forward or take action. For leaders who have trouble delegating, submission is something they need to practice more and more. When a leader does not delegate, the remove a developmental opportunity from others around them they can submit or delegate to. Submission is not a bad thing, but it needs to be practiced at the right time.

Omission is also a trait that is not often used when leadership is discussed. I see omission as being the practice of knowing what you should not do as well as what you should be doing. One of the key points in strategy is just this, knowing what you should pursue as well as what to say No to. Great leaders can selectively omit opportunities that deter from the focus that their teams or organizations will need in order to be successful. How often have you seen a leader take on a cause or initiative that spreads their limited resources to projects that are not in the current focus or strategy? I think this is a common occurrence and one that needs to be addressed sooner versus later.

Commission, Submission and Omission are key attributes for every leader to have. Knowing when to use each of them is even more important!

You have to keep learning

I love to learn and I can think back to my learning experiences with great joy in most cases. One of the most important things I have learned about learning is that most learning takes place in non-classroom situations. Ironically, I learned this tidbit of data while in a classroom at Peabody College of Vanderbilt University in either 1995 or 1996 while completing a Master's Degree in Human Resource Development. Malcolm Knowles, known as the "Father of Adult Learning" had done substantial research on how people learn and one of the summaries of his research is shown below:

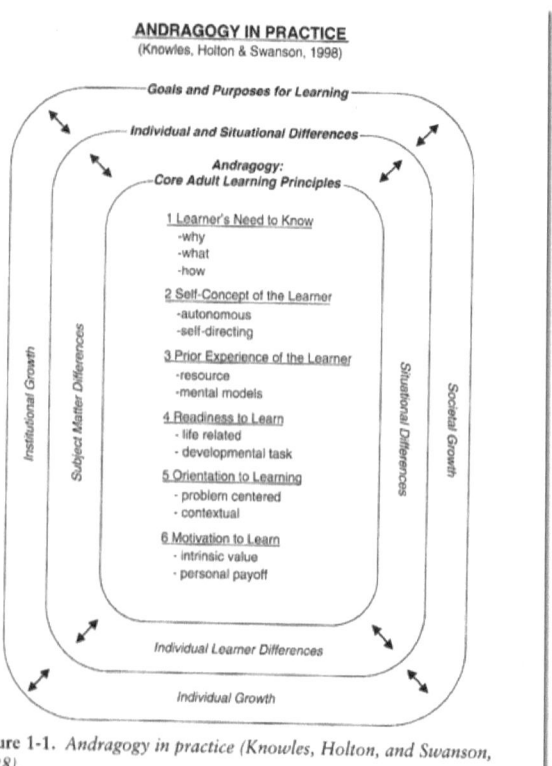

Figure 1-1. *Andragogy in practice (Knowles, Holton, and Swanson, 1998).*

I completed that degree in 1996 and have kept on learning since then, with most of this learning taking place in real-life work situations where the context of the situation gave grounding to the knowledge and information I was gaining.

I'll share a few of my most pertinent, if not painful, learning experiences below so you can gain a better understanding of how we learn outside of the classroom:

- In 1983 I learned that what may first appear to be a bad break can be a good break. This occurred when I was laid off from my first job. By being out of work this allowed me to spend the last 8 days of my father's life by his side. Even though there was no income coming in, the experience to be with my father is one I still cherish to this day.
- In 1987 I learned that not everything I hear needs to be repeated, and it may not even be true. This occurred when I heard that one of my co-workers was about to be laid off during a downsizing. I approached her to express my sorrow, and she looked very surprised to hear that she would be losing her job. About 15 minutes later her boss paid me a visit and instructed me to keep my mouth shut when I heard rumors that may be unsubstantiated. A painful, yet valuable, experience was gained that day. I have never forgotten this, although I still can have a big mouth.
- From 1990 through 1996 I learned that perseverance is a good habit to gain. This was learned while I was first a volunteer, and then an employee, of the <u>YMCA</u> in the

Nashville, TN area. I helped form a group that ultimately resulted in the formation of a new YMCA in a community that had a tremendous need for this kind of enterprise. I am proud to say today that this YMCA continues to flourish, and it makes me smile to meet other volunteers and staff members who have been involved and been changed by the presence of the Y in that community.

- From 2006 until now I am learning that there is value in taking risks. This began when I gave up my paying job with tremendous benefits to enter the search and consulting world. There was great security in the role I left, but my passion was to help organizations find and develop individuals to help them grow and flourish. I also learned that people buy primarily from people, based on trust and integrity. While I have certainly had my failures during this time, the highs far surpass the lows and I feel that God has continued to bless me in the work I do by putting so many interesting and engaging people in my path, both as colleagues and as clients.

I could go on, but that is enough for today.

I would challenge each of you to reflect on your own life and identify those times when you have learned outside the traditional constraints of the classroom. I suspect you will gain great insight into who you are and what you value by doing so.

Your most important network

I have written and read many an article about networking. These articles have pointed out the value of keeping in touch and many of them will also go into the finer points of which networks to focus on and why they are of value. I am not here today to dispel any of these articles or thoughts, but I am here to point out that there is one key network I read little about and I propose that this network is the most important of all of them. The most important network is your family. How you define family is up to you, but let me define family in my sense of the word in the context of this post.

I had the good fortune to grow up in an environment where I knew most of my aunts and uncles on my father's side of the family quite well. My dad was the middle child with two older sisters and two younger sisters. When you add this up I had about 28 in my generation, with 26 of them living to adulthood. Of these 26, 22 of us lived within a one block area at one time or another in our lives. The eldest in my cohort was born in 1943 and the youngest was born in 1968. That gives us a span over 3 generations and the stories and relationships among us are numerous.

As you can well imagine, the enclave has moved on and we are now spread across the country. I have cousins in Maine, New Jersey, South

Carolina, Florida and many other parts of the country. It is extremely rare that all of us are in the same place at the same time. The sad part of this is that we most often see one another now in a somewhat sad setting, the funeral of one of us.

This is the context of my post today. We have lost two in our group so far this year, with one of them being my brother and another being a cousin who passed away last weekend. It is sad to see one of our family members pass away, but the positive side is that it does provide an incentive for us to gather, greet and reminisce about not only the good old times, but to also talk about how we can continue to stay in touch.

So today I will get behind the wheel and make the 400 mile drive to my original hometown, nestled in the heart of the Midwest in the central part of Illinois. When I arrive I will see not only the past, but I will also see the present and the future.

Each one of us has a network in our family that we need to nurture and cherish. Too often I have missed opportunities to gain from this, but today I will not pass up that chance. While we will grieve the loss of one of our number, we will also smile, toast and celebrate the parents and relatives who have made us who we are today.

Take the time to stay in touch with your friends and loved ones. While it may seem awkward at times to talk with those you have not seen in years, the words will come and the bonds will never be broken.

Have a great day and take the time to connect with your family now while you have the chance.

From Telescopes to Microscopes, Great Leaders need it all

I have written before about the places I get ideas and inspiration for what I write here. Once again I give credit to my pastor and friend, David Cassidy, for helping me think about leadership in a different and descriptive manner. Today's post will look at the differing types of vision that leaders need to have in order to be successful. I enjoy learning from others and try to always give credit where it is due. To David I say "thank you" once more.

Great leaders need to be like chameleons. This does not mean that they are always changing in order to hide, but it does mean they are always changing and adapting. Leaders are about change and some of the situations that leaders encounter might cause the faint of heart to pull back and try to fade into the surroundings. Here are just a few of the challenges that great leaders may face:

- Helping companies grow
- Working with companies as they downsize
- Merger and Acquisition situations
- Bringing new products or services on line
- Establishing new products or services in a new area or market
- Reinforcing or changing company culture
- Pairing back or redirecting resources

Each of the situations above involve change and Leaders must excel at change. Change involves vision of many types and this is where the telescope and microscope analogy comes into play. Let's talk a few moments about telescopic and microscopic leadership tactics and strategy for leaders.

Telescopes are devices that enable us to see a long distance away. Leaders are often charged with the work of seeing not just what tomorrow holds, but also in seeing what may confront us in 6, 12, 24 or more months into the future. Having a good telescope has enabled many leaders to avoid pitfalls that may take things off track and this same telescopic vision will also enable the leader to see where the calm seas may life as they direct the organizational vessel into the future. Without this telescopic vision, the leader and the organization may fail, or fail to live up to their ultimate potential.

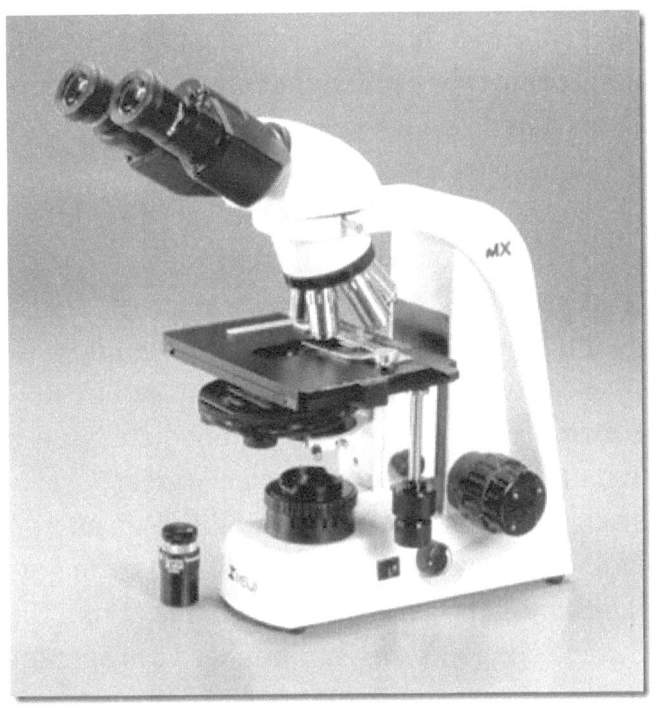

Microscopes are devices that enable one to see things at a much smaller level than can be done with the naked eye. Leaders also need this microscopic vision to get "into the weeds" to see why things are not functioning in the right manner after or during the time they are guiding the ship in this future direction. Great leaders have the ability to shift from telescopic to microscopic vision quite quickly and they also understand when to use one and not the other.

The inability to shift from telescopic to microscopic is one pitfall that many leaders have not mastered. I have seen many leaders, including yours truly, who have mastered the microscopic approach, but often have forgotten how to develop or utilize the telescopic approach. This leader does a good job of handling today's issues, but falters when it comes to casting a future vision and leading the team or organization past the immediate issue at hand. Likewise, some leaders have great telescopic vision, but lack the ability to drop into the weeds to "get under the hood" and fix major organizational issues. Always looking at the future keeps good leaders from becoming great leaders because they have not built enough organizational capacity for the longer journey ahead.

Great leaders need the ability to look ahead and also deal with today's issues. They require both telescopic and microscopic vision. Having the ability to use both, and understanding when to use either, is a key attribute that differentiates good leaders from those who will be great leaders.

I'll be back soon to talk more about how to develop your telescopic and microscopic leadership attributes.

Your Web of Inclusion-Who is there?

Just like a spider, we all spin webs. A spider spins his or her web to catch prey for survival needs. Our web is for survival also, but we don't have to kill our victims, thank heavens!

Each of us has many different webs that we spin. Some of mine include:

- executive search-my work in the search world puts me into contact with a variety of firms and individuals from varying walks of life and a myriad of industries; I enjoy the diversity and each one brings a different view and perspective
- leadership-I have had the opportunity to be a leader in a variety of settings, both paid and unpaid; the ability to lead from the front or even from the side or behind allows me to gain a better perspective into what I do well and where I need to improve
- career transition-I have been blessed to come into contact with so many who are on the journey from one career/job to another; this ministry has allowed me to gain a better perspective on my own career and to also see how others approach and overcome a

variety of issues or challenges in their own search
- fellow believers in Jesus- being part of a body of believers has enabled me to overcome temptations that might cause the individual to succumb to the challenges of everyday life; while I am not perfect, I can say that the many strands of a body and the small group we belong to only strengthen my resolve to try and live my life in a way that serves others
- Sigma Chi-I became a part of this international brotherhood in 1978 and I have never regretted my membership; there have been times I may have been disappointed in the behavior I personally have had, or the behavior of a fellow brother, but that fellowship, united by the Jordan Standard, allows me to realize that through Sigma Chi, I will find it here

There are others, but I think these will give you the picture.

Have you assumed the correct Leadership Position?

Leadership is such an interesting topic, one that I speak on and talk about often. I have also had the opportunity to practice this art and science in many episodes of my life, even now.

Leadership position is a crucial issue to consider and I think it is something that many leaders don't give enough attention to. My intent today is to speak about the most common types of leadership positioning and comment on when to assume each of these.

When I think of leadership position, I think of these most common places to lead from:

- leading from the front-my assumption is that most of us think of leaders being the person who is in front, making the charge; the lead dog in the pack, the one taking all of the risks and encouraging the group to keep moving; the biggest challenge with frontal leaders is that they can sometimes lose sight of their followers and they may turn around and see that no one is behind them

- leading from the side-leading from the side is an important role and this is needed in cases where the group or team needs someone to guide them, but not necessarily pull them; the sideline leader can almost be a "player coach" who participates in the work of the group while working to develop others to lead in the future-sideline leaders can be hampered when they have a group that is not mature enough for this style and who might lose sight of the goal or lose energy when they need to keep moving
- leading from the rear-this is the style that I think many have difficulty with; leading from the rear is almost a mentoring style of leadership and this kind of leader can provide great insight and wisdom for a team that has other emerging leaders who need a sounding board or a resource as they continue to stretch their wings-back seat leaders such as this type can be hampered if they act too much or act too little; there is a lot of "feel"

> involved, almost intuition, to measure the needs of the group and respond accordingly

Leadership is situational (thank you Ken Blanchard and Spencer Johnson) and knowing the needs of the group and the needs of the situation will dictate just which of these three styles to engage.

Gaining Wisdom from Others-The Art of Listening

Wisdom is often confused with data and knowledge, but wisdom is very different from either of these two items. Let me spend a little time first explaining the difference and I'll then get to the focus of the post.

Data is information, gathered in any number of ways. We all gather data daily, with some of this data being qualitative (descriptive) and other being quantitative (numerical). Data is a great asset to have in any circumstance, but it is only the beginning.

Data can be used to generate information. Information comes from taking data and seeing where the patterns lie. There may be correlations or relationships between items that occur and having the data will allow you to show causation or lack of such when the numbers are examined.

Knowledge comes from examining information over periods of time. Having information from one window of time is great, but you can learn much more by looking at information over greater spans of time or from varying sample sets such as geography and other factors.

- Wisdom is different. Wisdom may draw from data, information and knowledge, but wisdom is not any of these. Wisdom comes not just from the gathered data which is then reviewed and examined. Wisdom also comes from experience, and this is the key factor that makes wisdom so valuable when compared to the ingredients.

I compare wisdom to baking a cake. Let me explain.

Data could be the recipe, listing the ingredients or the list of the proper ingredients.

Information and knowledge will focus on how to combine the ingredients into differing types of cakes.

Wisdom comes from knowing which cake to bake and how you might adjust the recipe or the process based on factors learned from previous experiences. Baking a cake at low altitude is different than baking a cake at high altitude. Likewise, certain cakes are difficult to bake from scratch (take Angel Food for example) while others cakes are easy to bake from scratch. Some cakes are very rich and filling (pound cake) while others are much lighter.

Life provides us with data, information, knowledge and wisdom. Education typically focuses on the data, information and knowledge and often gives less focus to the wisdom realm. Some of the best wisdom I have gained has come from listening to those I know and respect. I'll focus on two people today to discuss this further. These two individuals are my mother and father in law. Listen closely and you may learn something.

My wife and I married over 32 years ago and we dated for 2 years prior to that. When someone gets married they gain more than a spouse, they gain a family. I have been so fortunate to gain so much from the family I joined when I married my wife.

Here is some of the wisdom I have gained from this journey:

- The days are long, but the years are short- As I have gotten older this has become readily apparent. While a young man I remember well the days when things drug along, but now I see how quickly time passes, especially from week to week, month to month and so on. Enjoy the day as it appears and learn from the present.

- Buy a white car-This may seem simple, but there is a deeper meaning here. We all have systems or organizations we are part of and they all require maintaining to keep them in running order. The value of an organization comes from both the internal and external appearance and making things simple to maintain is of the essence. White cars are easy to keep clean, so make your organization a "white car" by being transparent and keeping things in shape and clean. This could also delve to the area of Lean principles, but I'll pass on that today.

- "Nothing wrong with that one"-On the surface this makes little sense, but let me give you context, because wisdom is very context based. I learned years ago from my father in law that a good parking spot may have shade in the summer and usually always is away from other cars and is next to a boundary. By parking in these types of spots you can minimize the damage or wear and tear on your vehicle. You should manage your life in the same manner. Rather than spending times in situations that may cause damage, keep yourself in the safe lanes and avoid areas of obvious temptation that may lead to a "wreck" in your personal life. This may also involve parking near the lights when you park at night-nothing good happens in the dark unless you are with your loved ones, so travel in the safe lanes and park in the best spots. You'll be glad you did

- Take care of your vehicle-Again, this comes from my father in law and his passion for keeping his car clean. This relates closely to the previously mentioned Lean principles in the last segment. Keep what you need, keep it clean and get rid of what you don't need. One of the signs that we live in a society where this is not practiced is the growth of storage buildings (next segment)

- The world is being taken over by storage buildings-This remark comes from my mother in law and it shows the effect of a society that clings too much to the material and not enough to the value of people and relationships. If we need to store things away from where we live, this usually means we have too much stuff and we need to get rid of it. Our society is full of solutions to problems that do not exist. If you need something, buy it. When you don't need it anymore, sell it or give it away. Why keep what you don't need.

I could go on and share more, but I think this is a good start to sharing the wisdom I have gained from a series of relationships that have grown over the last 34 years.

What wisdom have you gained in your life journey?

Are you spending time with those who can help you gain wisdom?

Are you sharing your wisdom with others?

Take the time to listen well to those you know, trust and love. The wisdom will come.

Putting the Pieces into Place-The Challenge of Networking

Networking is one of my favorite topics and it is also one of the areas where I spend a lot of my time and effort. Networking is an essential practice for all business leaders and I give credit to our success, or failure, as a business based on our ability to network with the right people in the right place at the appropriate time.

Earlier in my life I was a compulsive puzzle person and I still enjoy a good puzzle now and then. I remember well the day when our children were younger when I would set up a large puzzle on a table and we would all work on this together. I have also been prone to work on a crossword puzzle or two and Sudoku is an interesting puzzle pastime that I also enjoy.

With most puzzles like those listed above you can have a very clear picture of the intended result prior to beginning the process. Every jigsaw puzzle includes a photo of the finished scene and crossword puzzles are either "right or wrong" when you finish, with Sudoku being the same. Networking puzzles are not like this and that is an important distinction to remember when you start out on your networking path. You may have a specific target or outcome in mind when you begin a networking process, but you also need to understand how to flex or redirect your efforts when the next piece of the puzzle is something you did not expect. I will say more about how to do this below and in a future post.

I got started in the Talent Acquisition and Talent Development world about 9 years ago and I have the good fortune to have some great mentors who helped me with the strategy of how to get started. Some of the early thoughts I had included the following:

- Who do I know?
- What services might I provide for them?
- What is the probability that they would consider me credible to provide this service for their firm?

These three variables helped me generate the initial map for concentrating my efforts in building the business. I started with those I knew and with things I also had credibility in providing. In the puzzle nomenclature I started with a clear picture in my mind of the who, what and how before I ever stepped foot outside the door.

Life changed that picture in many ways and here are just a few of these detours and dead ends:

- Firms already had a good source for the services I provided
- Our method of providing services (retained search) was not the method they chose to employ (they used contingency search)

- There was no need for Talent Development at the time I called upon them

These items could be a huge chasm to some, but they only allowed me to re-craft the final picture. The key thing I always try to remember about networking is that there is always a value I can provide and be provided when I meet with someone else. People are like onions, meaning that they have many layers of influence. What you see on the surface is not the only thing to consider. Just because someone does not appear to have the connection or influence you first think, people have many other layers of connectivity when you get past the first layer. Here are a few examples of what I mean from personal experience:

- One of our newest clients was referred to us by someone who knew of our work in the area-many of our clients come from referrals; the moral here is that you never know when you are "interviewing" for your next role, so always do your best, no matter the circumstances

- Clients come from places you would never imagine; I have had clients come from LinkedIn, church and many other activities I currently or formerly participated in

- I spend a lot of time in the industries where we do work; being connected to leaders in the areas we focus on helps to give us credibility and it also shows we are willing to give back to the professions we serve

I'll stop here today and pick up next week with some more ideas about how you might complete some of the networking puzzles you might be working one.

Always check the floor, you never know when an important piece may have slipped out of view.

Don't let a First Impression Sidetrack a Potential Connection

Networking is a constant activity in my world and my recent trip to India provided many opportunities to network with individuals and companies I would not normally have a chance to meet with. I had the chance to meet with people from countries such as Dubai, Italy, Australia, Malaysia and of course India during my visit. One such encounter has stuck in my mind since I returned over two weeks ago and I plan to learn as much from this as I possibly can. I'll share it with you also.

While traveling abroad provides many opportunities to meet with others, it can also be more than a little taxing on the body and the mind. While in India I slept an average of four to five hours per day and not all of those were in the typically night time hours where I was. As a result of this amended sleeping schedule there were times in the day when I might be a little dull.

One of the evenings while in Mumbai I was having dinner with a few of my fellow speaker colleagues and a local leader in the world of higher education. It was the end of a busy day and I was a little worn out. Our host was a high-energy individual who had enough energy for all of us. Toward the end of our dinner engagement he looked at me and said "Dan, it has been a pleasure talking with you even though you are a little benign." Benign? I have been called many things in my life, but that was a first.

If my host had taken into account that there were few gaps in the conversation with to interject a thought, coupled with the fact that all of us other than him were in completely different time zones he might have phrased his comment in a different manner.

What did I learn from this exchange? I learned the following:

- When talking with others, always allow time for others to speak

- When meeting with a group, even though you may have overwhelming interest in one member of the group, do not let that monopolize the conversation

- Be careful to use words when describing others that may be taken in a negative manner

- Consider the situation before passing judgment on another's behaviors

I have had many a good laugh with my other colleagues when we talk about this dinner conversation. If anything, I am probably the least "benign" person you will encounter. Circumstances dictated that I play a background role in this case.

Networking with others, especially with those from other cultures, can provide a great platform to learn and grow. Be careful to use words or make assumptions that may be misunderstood by others in the group.

The Best Talent Development Opportunities may Surprise you

Talent Development and Talent Acquisition are the two areas where I spend the bulk of my time, both personally and professionally. I am fortunate to have a business where I am blessed to do what I do well and get paid to do it. Some are not that fortunate, but I am extremely thankful for the opportunity to do what I do. The "day job" here at Ryan Search & Consulting is what most people see above the surface, but an equally important and rewarding part of what I do is contained in the work I am fortunate to be a part of on Monday nights (and throughout the week) with the Career Transition Support Group at Brentwood United Methodist Church in Brentwood, TN.

Today's post will focus more on the development side and I'll take more of an organic approach to what we will talk about. The word organic is one that has grown in usage and emphasis in the last two decades with the growing emphasis on healthy foods on the part of many. Organic is also a word I use when describing the development process that many of us go through in our personal and professional lives. We all go through multiple growing seasons in our lives. These seasons involve a preparation, cultivation and harvesting process. I suspect many of you can recount times in your life when you have gone through preparation, cultivation and harvest in your own careers.

The interesting thing about this process is that not all species go through the same type of process, and some of us will bloom when you least expect it. I have a couple of examples to share from the plant world and I'll then shift to how this might apply to the world of leadership and development.

Lycoris squamigera is also known as the Resurrection Lily or "Surprise Lily". This plant will grow in the springtime, die back and then miraculously reappear in the summertime with beautiful blooms that occur when you might least expect them.

Schlumbergera, or "Christmas Cactus" is a species that originates in Brazil and tends to bloom in the late fall around Thanksgiving or Christmas. While many blooming flowers and plants show their beauty in the warmer months, this plant chooses to impress us in a less than typical time, especially for us in the northern hemisphere.

The two plants above represent plants or types that provide beauty and pleasure at times when you might least expect them to. So too, we see others in our world who have the capacity to do the same if we only don't give up on them. Too often we expect all of our staff members or co-workers to go through the same cycle of development that we may have experienced on our own. While many of us may "flower" or produce on schedule during the normal seasons of our career, there are others who will produce or hit their peak when you least expect it.

The moral to the story for today is to not assume that each and every species you have in the workplace will react and develop, or grow, on the same timetable. Some will harvest when you expect them to, some will never produce, and still some others will take your breath away when they come forth with outstanding ideas or actions when you least expect it.

Biologists know their species when they work with them and leaders need to know their staff members too. Don't expect every member of your team to produce at the same time, even if you put them through the same cultivation process. Some will bloom right on cue, but some will never do so and the final group, those we are highlighting today, will overwhelm you when you least expect it.

The second message is to never stop cultivating those around you. While some will require more attention, some will require less, and almost all will produce some fruit if you just stick with them.

Are you a Chronos or Kairos Leader?

If you read my blog often you will notice that I get a lot of my inspiration from my pastor, David Cassidy, at Christ Community Church in Franklin, TN. David is a great speaker and a well-read individual who has an uncanny way to put concepts into words that catch my attention and make me think. For that, I am most thankful.

During yesterday's sermon, David discussed the concept of Chronos versus Kairos when talking about time. Here is a short description of each:

- Chronos is a sequential methodology of describing time, an orderly fashion
- Kairos is more like a unique moment, even THE unique moment for things to occur

While hearing the difference between chronos and Kairos it made me think about leadership and management. I see a strong connection between these two terms and how leaders lead and managers manage. I would even go so far as to say that there are also chronos leaders. More to come on that concept. Let's take a moment today and look at how these concepts lend themselves to the concept of leading and managing others.

Chronos looks at time in a more sequential and orderly fashion. From a chronos perspective, there is an order to things and getting things in that order is of great importance. There is also a quantitative component to chronos.

Chronos thinking, or chronos leadership, is more about getting things into an orderly fashion, getting them in sequence and realizing that there are quantitative (numerical) measures that need to take place in order for success to occur. Chronos leadership is important. Things need to be in order and need to be sequential in most cases for things to happen as they should. When I think of chronos leadership I think of project management. Project Management is very much about chronos leadership. The successful project is very sequential with measures in many places and time frames being of great value. Without chronos leaders, projects will fail.

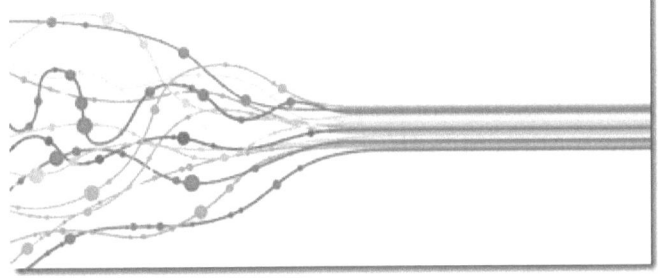

Kairos leaders are different. Kairos leaders are more about "carpe minutam" (seize the minute or moment). Kairos leaders will think less about the sequence or the cost, but they will take a more intuitive approach and realize that there are unique times when things come together in a unique way for success to occur. Kairos leadership is not opposed to chronos leadership, but it is different in how it occurs. Many of the great events in history have occurred due to Kairos leadership, and many more have occurred due to a combination of chronos and Kairos leadership working hand in hand.

Dwight Eisenhower was a chronos leader. He worked with others, specifically George C. Marshall, to plan to D-Day invasion in June 1944 by sequencing thousands of events in order to make sure that this invasion of Europe was successful. Even with all of this planning, he resorted to Kairos leadership in choosing the invasion date, June 6. By keeping up with the weather reports he used his chronos skills to find the right window and then he made the decision to move forward on June 6, primarily with his Kairos skills. He even went so far as to write a letter of apology for the failure of the invasion in case things did not go right, which was truly a combination of both chronos and Kairos leadership.

David was a Kairos leader in the bible when he chose to fight the philistine, Goliath, on the battlefield. From a chronos perspective there was no way that David could slay the giant. Using his Kairos thinking, he chose the small, smooth stones and used his sling to defeat the obvious winner, at least from a chronos perspective.

Consider these two quotes that reflect chronos vs. Kairos leadership:

- ***In preparing for battle I have always found that plans are useless, but planning is indispensable.***

  Dwight D. Eisenhower (source: Brainyquote.com)

- ***Everyone here has the sense that right now is one of those moments*** *when we are influencing the future.*

Steve Jobs (source: Brainyquote.com)

www.ingramcontent.com/pod-product-compliance
Lightning Source LLC
Chambersburg PA
CBHW021017180526
45163CB00005B/1999